Fields of
FLAVOUR

Sarina Jacobson

First published in 2002 by Struik Publishers
(a division of New Holland Publishing (South Africa) (Pty) Ltd)
Cornelis Struik House, 80 McKenzie Street, Cape Town 8001
www.struik.co.za

New Holland Publishing is a member of the Johnnic Publishing Group

10 9 8 7 6 5 4 3 2 1

PUBLISHING MANAGER: Linda de Villiers
EDITOR: Joy Clack
DESIGNER: Beverley Dodd
PHOTOGRAPHER: Dirk Pieters
STYLIST: Abigail Donnelly

With thanks to the following for supplying props:
LIM, L'Orangerie, Loft Living, Pieter Visser Interiors, Summer House and Plush Bazaar.

Reproduction by Hirt and Carter Cape (Pty) Ltd
Printed and bound by Sing Cheong Printing
  Company Limited

ISBN 1 86872 680 0

A NOTE FROM THE AUTHOR

Food is a language of its own. The individual ingredients are the words and their interrelationships form the shape and poetry of the sentence, the recipe.

An understanding of the basic properties of each ingredient is vital to the cooking process. But more important is the development of a strong sensory relationship with each ingredient. This gives you the artistic licence to experiment and enjoy cooking as an exciting sensual experience rather than a domestic burden.

It is in this spirit that I dedicate this book to my grandmother Sarina Illos, who spoke to me in this language and taught me to appreciate the poetry in taste.

My special thanks to: Tevia Rosmarin, Linzi Rabinowitz and Phillippa Cheifitz for their help and support.

SARINA JACOBSON

CONTENTS

INTRODUCTION

There are two imperatives that apply to preparing healthy and enjoyable vegetarian meals. These are nutrition and to preserve and enhance taste. Although most people believe nutritious food is vital for their wellbeing, many equate such nutritious foods as bland or tasteless. This book attempts to prove that food can be both tasty and healthy. I believe both are equally important and I have used cooking methods specifically aimed at achieving dishes that are both delicious and nourishing. The methods used comprise four main processes: blanching, baking, roasting and steaming.

Blanching entails plunging vegetables into boiling water for a short while. Here the time the vegetable is in the water is critical, as the longer it stays in the water the more it loses both flavour and nutritional content. Although raw vegetables are highest in nutritional content, they are often difficult to eat and hard to digest. Blanching is the best way to retain nutritional value and flavour, while also making the food easy to digest.

A quicker method is to cover the vegetables with boiling water, leave them to stand until they turn bright in colour, then drain.

Baking entails placing vegetables in a casserole-type dish with seasoning and spices and very little oil or sauce, and allowing the vegetables to cook in their own juices. When the vegetables are soft you can add additional spices and/or sauces before reheating.

Roasting entails brushing the vegetables with a little oil and seasoning and spices, and placing them on a baking sheet, which is also brushed with oil, to roast. Roast at 150 °C (300 °F) until the vegetables are crispy.

Steaming (right) entails placing vegetables in a layered steaming pot that has boiling water beneath it. Allow the vegetables to steam until they are tender but still crunchy.

INTRODUCTION

SOUPS

Soup can be a simple meal on its own, especially when legumes, grains and a variety of vegetables are combined in one recipe.

MOST SOUPS REQUIRE

1. a vegetable soup stock, which can be in the form of a cube or a powder (both to be dissolved in water), or the water left after blanching vegetables; and

2. a soup base comprising onion, garlic, soup celery, carrots, sea salt, coarsely ground black pepper and fructose.

LENTIL AND VEGETABLE SOUP

15 ml (1 Tbsp) sunflower oil

1 medium onion, finely diced

2 cloves garlic, crushed

a pinch of sea salt

4 sticks soup celery (stalks and leaves), finely chopped

60 ml (¼ cup) fresh coriander, finely chopped

a pinch of coarsely ground black pepper

2 medium carrots, peeled and diced

1 large potato, peeled and diced

125 ml (½ cup) peeled and diced butternut

125 ml (½ cup) diced courgettes (baby marrows)

a pinch of ground cumin

a pinch of ground leaf masala

a pinch of ground turmeric

1 litre (4 cups) soup stock

250 ml (1 cup) black or red lentils, cooked (see page 74)

a pinch of fructose

Heat the oil and fry the onion, garlic and salt in a saucepan over low heat until translucent. Add the celery, coriander and black pepper. Cover with a lid and continue cooking on low until the celery is tender. Add the vegetables and spices, and stir for a few minutes before adding the stock.

Bring the soup to the boil, then immediately reduce heat and simmer on low until all the vegetables are tender.

Use a potato masher to crush the vegetables a little, then stir in the lentils and fructose. If you prefer a thin soup, add more water, or simmer a little longer to allow the vegetables and the lentils to form a thick soup. Set the soup aside for a while. Reheat just before serving.

SERVES 4

SPLIT PEA, BARLEY AND VEGETABLE SOUP

250 ml (1 cup) green split peas

125 ml (½ cup) pearl barley

875 ml (3½ cups) water

1 ml (¼ tsp) sea salt

15 ml (1 Tbsp) sunflower oil

1 large onion, finely diced

2 cloves garlic, crushed

a pinch of sea salt

4 sticks soup celery (stalks and leaves), finely chopped

a pinch of fresh or dried sage

a pinch of coarsely ground black pepper

2 carrots, peeled and finely diced

1 large potato, peeled and finely diced

250 ml (1 cup) peeled and finely diced butternut

1–1.25 litres (4–5 cups) soup stock

a pinch of fructose

Bring the peas, barley and water to the boil. Reduce heat, add the salt and simmer over low heat until cooked. Set aside.

Heat the oil and fry the onion, garlic and salt in a saucepan until translucent. Add the celery, sage and pepper. Cover with a lid and cook on low until the celery is tender.

Add the carrots, potato and butternut and stir for a few minutes before adding the stock. Bring the soup to the boil, then reduce heat immediately and simmer until the vegetables are soft.

Stir in the split peas, barley and fructose.

Leave the soup to stand for a while. Reheat just before serving.

SERVES 4

CHICKPEA AND VEGETABLE SOUP

15 ml (1 Tbsp) olive oil

1 large onion, cut into large pieces

2 cloves garlic, crushed

a pinch of sea salt

4 sticks soup celery (stalks and leaves),
cut into large pieces

2 ml (¼ tsp) fresh chilli, seeded and crushed

60 ml (¼ cup) fresh coriander, finely chopped

a pinch of ground cumin

2 carrots, peeled and cut into large chunks

1 large potato, peeled and cut into large chunks

2 courgettes (baby marrows), cut into large chunks

250 ml (1 cup) peeled and cubed pumpkin

1–1.25 litres (4–5 cups) soup stock

250 ml (1 cup) chickpeas, cooked (see page 74)

a pinch of ground cinnamon

a pinch of ground turmeric or saffron

a pinch of fructose

fresh coriander leaves to garnish

Heat the oil and fry the onion, garlic and salt in a saucepan on low until translucent. Add the celery, chilli, coriander and cumin. Cover with a lid and continue cooking on low until the celery is tender. Add the vegetables and stir for a few minutes before adding the soup stock.

Bring the soup to the boil. Reduce heat immediately and simmer on low until the vegetables have softened.

Add the chickpeas, spices and fructose and mix. Add water to thin the soup – its consistency is generally watery. Let the soup stand for a while. Reheat just before serving. Garnish with fresh coriander leaves.

This soup can be served on its own or over a bed of couscous.

SERVES 4

SOUPS

BLACK-EYED BEAN AND VEGETABLE SOUP

30 ml (2 Tbsp) olive oil

1 large onion, finely diced

2 cloves garlic, crushed

a pinch of sea salt

4 sticks soup celery (stalks and leaves), finely chopped

a pinch of fresh or dried mixed herbs

125 ml (½ cup) peeled and finely diced carrots

125 ml (½ cup) peeled and finely diced potato

125 ml (½ cup) finely diced courgettes (baby marrows)

125 ml (½ cup) peeled and finely diced butternut

125 ml (½ cup) skinned and finely chopped fresh ripe tomatoes

1–1.25 litres (4–5 cups) soup stock

a pinch of coarsely ground black pepper

a pinch of ground leaf masala

5 ml (1 tsp) fructose

60 ml (¼ cup) fresh coriander, finely chopped

250 ml (1 cup) black-eyed beans, cooked (see page 74)

Heat the oil and fry the onions, garlic and salt in a saucepan until translucent. Add the celery and mixed herbs. Cover with a lid and cook on low until the celery is tender.

Add the vegetables and stir for a few minutes before adding the stock. Bring the soup to the boil, then reduce heat immediately and simmer on low until the vegetables are soft.

Stir in the pepper, masala, fructose and coriander. Add the beans and mix. Let the soup stand for a while. Reheat just before serving.

SERVES 4

BUTTERNUT AND RICE SOUP

30 ml (2 Tbsp) sunflower oil
1 large onion, finely diced
2 cloves garlic, crushed
2 leeks, finely diced
a pinch of sea salt
a pinch of ground cumin
2 sticks soup celery, finely chopped
500 ml (2 cups) baked and mashed butternut
180 ml (¾ cup) basmati rice, cooked (see page 60)
1–1.25 litres (4–5 cups) soup stock
60 ml (¼ cup) fresh coriander, finely chopped
a pinch of coarsely ground black pepper
a pinch of ground leaf masala
a pinch of turmeric
a pinch of fructose
1 x 400 ml can coconut milk

Heat the oil and fry the onion, garlic, leeks and salt in a saucepan until translucent. Add the cumin and celery. Cover with a lid and cook on low until the leeks and celery are tender.

Add the butternut, rice and stock. Cover and simmer on low for 15 minutes, stirring occasionally.

Add the coriander, spices, fructose and half of the coconut milk, stirring slowly. Add more milk for a thinner consistency. Set aside.

Reheat just before serving.

SERVES 4

SOYA CREAM OF BROCCOLI SOUP

30 ml (2 Tbsp) olive oil
1 large onion, finely diced
2 cloves garlic, crushed
a pinch of sea salt
a pinch of dried sage
500 ml (2 cups) soya milk
500 ml (2 cups) broccoli florets, blanched
1 vegetable stock cube dissolved in
250 ml (1 cup) boiling water
a pinch of coarsely ground black pepper
a pinch of sea salt
a pinch of fructose
60 ml (¼ cup) soya cream

Heat the oil and fry the onion, garlic, salt and sage in a saucepan until the onion is translucent. Reduce heat to low, then add the soya milk. Stir and set aside.

Place the broccoli into a blender. Add the soup stock, pepper, salt and fructose. Add the onion and milk mixture and blend on a low speed so as not to separate the milk.

Pour the soup back into the pot and reheat. Add the cream once the mixture is very hot. Stir well and serve immediately.

SERVES 4

SOUPS

SOYA CREAM OF VEGETABLE SOUP

30 ml (2 Tbsp) sunflower oil
1 large onion, finely diced
2 cloves garlic, crushed
2 leeks, finely diced
a pinch of sea salt
2 sticks soup celery (stalks and leaves), finely chopped
a pinch of fresh or dried mixed herbs
2 carrots, peeled and diced
6 cauliflower florets
10 fine green bean stalks, diced
2 courgettes (baby marrows), diced
1 litre (4 cups) soup stock
1 large potato, peeled and cooked
a pinch of coarsely ground black pepper
a pinch of fructose
180 ml (¾ cup) soya cream

Heat the oil and fry the onion, garlic, leeks and salt in a saucepan until the onion is translucent. Stir in the celery and mixed herbs. Cover with a lid and cook on low until the celery and leeks are tender.

In the meantime, blanch the carrots, cauliflower, beans and marrows, and drain.

Place the onion and leek mixture into a blender. Add the blanched vegetables, stock, potato, black pepper and fructose, and blend. Add more stock if a thinner soup is desired.

Pour the soup back into the pot and reheat. Add the cream to the soup when it is hot and stir well.

SERVES 4

THAI SWEET POTATO AND BUTTERNUT SOUP

375 ml (1½ cups) peeled and roasted butternut

375 ml (1½ cups) peeled and roasted sweet potato

500 ml (2 cups) soup stock

½ small onion, diced

2 cloves garlic

2 ml (¼ tsp) fresh chilli, seeded and crushed

60 ml (¼ cup) fresh coriander, chopped

3 ml (½ tsp) fructose

3 ml (½ tsp) soy sauce

3 ml (½ tsp) peeled and grated fresh ginger

1 x 400 ml can coconut milk

a pinch of sea salt

60 ml (¼ cup) finely chopped spring onion to garnish

Mash the butternut and sweet potatoes together and place them in a pot. Add the stock, bring it to the boil, then reduce heat and simmer.

Place the onion, garlic, chilli, coriander, fructose, soy sauce and ginger into a blender and blend. Add the mixture to the soup and stir.

Add the coconut milk and salt and stir.

Add more stock if the consistency is too thick. Set aside.

Reheat slowly over medium heat so as not to curdle the coconut milk. Garnish with spring onion and serve immediately.

SERVES 4

CHUNKY MISO SOUP

15 ml (1 Tbsp) toasted sesame oil

2 spring onions, finely diced

125 ml (½ cup) finely grated carrot

125 ml (½ cup) finely sliced button mushrooms

5 ml (1 tsp) crushed wakame seaweed

3 ml (½ tsp) soy sauce

1.5 litres (6 cups) water

1 block fresh tofu (about 100 g), finely diced

30 ml (2 Tbsp) pure miso paste

60 ml (¼ cup) boiling water

2 ml (¼ tsp) peeled and grated fresh ginger

Heat the oil in a saucepan and fry the spring onions, carrot, mushrooms, seaweed and soy sauce for about 5 minutes. Add the water and bring to the boil. Add the diced tofu and simmer over medium heat for a few minutes.

In the meantime, dilute the miso in the boiling water with the ginger. When it has formed a smooth paste, stir it into the soup.

Serve immediately.

SERVES 4

SOUPS

SALADS

The salads at *Fields* restaurant comprise mostly cooked vegetables and grains, most of which can be served and eaten hot.

AUBERGINE WAFERS WITH PEPPERS AND TOMATOES

30 ml (2 Tbsp) olive oil

2 medium onions, finely diced

5 cloves garlic, crushed

3 ml (½ tsp) sea salt

8 fresh ripe tomatoes, skinned and finely chopped

2 ml (¼ tsp) coarsely ground black pepper

15 ml (1 Tbsp) fructose

60 ml (¼ cup) fresh coriander, finely chopped

1 large green pepper, seeded and finely sliced

olive oil for roasting

a pinch of herb salt

2 large aubergines (brinjals), cut into thin rings and dégorged

750 ml (3 cups) sunflower oil for deep-frying

a few fresh coriander leaves and toasted pine kernels to garnish

Preheat the oven to 180 °C (350 °F).

Heat the olive oil and fry the onions, 3 cloves of garlic and salt in a saucepan until translucent. Add the tomatoes, pepper and fructose and bring to the boil. Reduce heat and simmer for 1 hour. Add the chopped coriander 15 minutes before the end of the cooking time.

Arrange the green pepper slices on a baking sheet, brush with olive oil and sprinkle with salt. Roast until softened.

In a deep frying pan or wok, deep-fry the aubergines until golden on both sides. Drain on a board covered in paper towel.

Spoon a layer of tomato sauce into a bowl. Alternate layers of tomato sauce, aubergines, garlic and green pepper. Garnish and serve.

SERVES 4

SALADS

BUTTERNUT, ROCKET, ORANGE AND ALMOND SALAD

SALAD

sunflower oil for roasting
1 large butternut, peeled and cubed
a pinch of herb salt
a pinch of ground cinnamon
a pinch of fructose
1 x 50 g packet fresh rocket
1 medium orange, peeled and cut into small pieces
125 ml (½ cup) roasted almonds

ORANGE DRESSING

125 ml (½ cup) orange juice
45 ml (3 Tbsp) fructose
1 drop almond essence
a pinch of herb salt

Preheat the oven to 150 °C (300 °F).

Brush a baking sheet with oil. Arrange the butternut on it and brush lightly with oil. Sprinkle with salt, cinnamon and fructose. Roast until golden.

To make the dressing, pour the orange juice and fructose into a small saucepan and simmer over medium heat, stirring until it thickens into a syrup. Remove from heat. Add the almond essence and herb salt and mix. Set aside.

Wash and dry the rocket leaves and scatter them and the orange pieces over a platter. Place the roasted butternut on top and sprinkle the almonds in between. Pour over the orange dressing.

SERVES 4

GREEN BEAN, CASHEW AND FETA SALAD

250 g fine green beans

15 ml (1 Tbsp) olive oil

1 small onion, finely diced

2 small cloves garlic, crushed

a pinch of sea salt

a pinch of fresh or dried mixed herbs

a pinch of coarsely ground black pepper

2 ml (¼ tsp) lemon juice

125 ml (½ cup) crumbled feta cheese

60 ml (¼ cup) roasted cashew nuts

Blanch the beans and drain.

Heat the oil and fry the onions, garlic and salt on low until translucent. Add the herbs, pepper and lemon juice and stir. Mix in the green beans. Cover with a lid and cook on low for 5 minutes. Remove from heat and empty into a deep dish. Add the feta cheese and cashew nuts and toss.

SERVES 4

ROASTED BEETROOT AND BABY CARROT SALAD

SALAD

500 ml (2 cups) fresh beetroot, peeled and cubed
150 g fresh baby carrots
sunflower oil for roasting
herb salt
finely chopped fresh parsley to garnish

DRESSING

5 ml (1 tsp) balsamic vinegar
5 ml (1 tsp) soy sauce
5 ml (1 tsp) apple juice
60 ml (¼ cup) water

Preheat the oven to 180 °C (350 °F).

Place the beetroot and the carrots on separate baking sheets. Brush lightly with oil and sprinkle with herb salt. Roast until tender.

To make the dressing, mix together the vinegar, soy sauce, apple juice and water.

When the vegetables are cooked, place them in a shallow salad bowl. Pour over the dressing and garnish with parsley.

SERVES 4

ROASTED CAULIFLOWER AND BROCCOLI WITH TAHINI

SALAD

olive oil for roasting

10 cauliflower florets

herb salt

10 broccoli florets

60 ml (¼ cup) toasted sesame seeds to garnish

TAHINI DRESSING

125 ml (½ cup) tahini

2 cloves garlic

a pinch of sea salt

a pinch of fructose

2 ml (¼ tsp) crushed cumin seeds

15 ml (1 Tbsp) finely chopped fresh coriander

15 ml (1 Tbsp) freshly squeezed lemon juice

300 ml (1¼ cups) water

Preheat the oven to 180 °C (350 °F).

First make the dressing by blending all the ingredients together in an electric blender until they form a smooth sauce.

Arrange the cauliflower florets on a baking sheet, brush lightly with oil and sprinkle with herb salt. Place in the oven to roast until golden.

Blanch the broccoli and drain. Mix the cauliflower and broccoli in a bowl. Add the tahini dressing and sesame seeds and toss. Transfer the salad to a salad bowl and serve.

SERVES 4

CRISPY TOFU AND MANGETOUT WITH CHILLI-PEANUT SAUCE

SALAD

500 ml (2 cups) sunflower oil for deep-frying
4 blocks fresh tofu (100 g each)
150 g fresh mangetout, halved
fresh coriander leaves to garnish

CHILLI-PEANUT SAUCE

125 ml (½ cup) crunchy peanut butter
2 cloves garlic, crushed
2 spring onions, finely chopped
15 ml (1 Tbsp) finely chopped fresh coriander
5 ml (1 tsp) fructose
3 ml (½ tsp) soy sauce
2 ml (¼ tsp) peeled and grated fresh ginger
¼ fresh green or red chilli, seeded and crushed
180 ml (¾ cup) coconut milk

First make the sauce by blending all the ingredients in an electric blender until creamy. For an even creamier texture, add more coconut milk.

Pour the oil into a wok and heat until sizzling. Cut the tofu into medium-sized cubes and plunge them into the oil until golden in colour. Remove and strain in a colander.

Blanch the mangetout and drain.

Place the tofu and mangetout into a salad bowl. Pour over the chilli-peanut sauce and garnish with fresh coriander leaves.

SERVES 4

ROASTED POTATOES AND GREEN BEAN SALAD

500 ml (2 cups) peeled and diced potatoes

olive oil for roasting

a pinch of sea salt

2 cloves garlic, crushed

a pinch of coarsely ground black pepper

5 ml (1 tsp) finely chopped fresh parsley

500 ml (2 cups) fine green beans, diced

3 ml (½ tsp) freshly squeezed lemon juice

2 ml (¼ tsp) fructose

125 ml (½ cup) toasted sunflower seeds

125 ml (½ cup) toasted pumpkin seeds

125 ml (½ cup) toasted sesame seeds

Preheat the oven to 180 °C (350 °F).

Place the potatoes onto a baking sheet and brush lightly with oil. Sprinkle over the salt, garlic, pepper and parsley. Place into the oven and roast until golden and crispy.

Blanch the beans in salted water.

Place the beans and potatoes into a bowl and toss in the lemon juice, fructose and seeds. Place onto a salad platter and serve.

SERVES 4

SALADS

THAI CASHEW, MUSHROOM AND RICE SALAD

15 ml (1 Tbsp) toasted sesame oil

15 ml (1 Tbsp) soy sauce

500 ml (2 cups) thinly sliced button mushrooms

60 ml (¼ cup) finely chopped spring onions

125 ml (½ cup) roasted salted cashew nuts

500 ml (2 cups) short-grain brown rice, cooked (see page 60)

2 cloves garlic, crushed

2 ml (¼ tsp) fresh chilli, seeded and crushed

2 ml (¼ tsp) peeled and grated fresh ginger

60 ml (¼ cup) fresh coriander, finely chopped

60 ml (¼ cup) coconut cream

2 ml (¼ tsp) fructose

2 ml (¼ tsp) herb salt

a pinch of ground lemon grass

a few fresh coriander leaves to garnish

Heat the oil and soy sauce in a deep frying pan or wok. Add the mushrooms and cook on low until all the liquid has evaporated.

Stir in the spring onions and cashews and fry gently on low for a few minutes. Remove from heat and set aside.

Place the cooked rice into a mixing bowl. Add the mushrooms, garlic, chilli, ginger, coriander, coconut cream, fructose, salt and lemon grass. Mix thoroughly and then transfer to a salad bowl.

Garnish with fresh coriander leaves and serve.

SERVES 4

TOASTED QUINOA AND CHICKPEA SALAD

500 ml (2 cups) cooked quinoa (see page 62)

250 ml (1 cup) cooked or canned chickpeas (see page 74)

olive oil for roasting

2 ml (¼ tsp) sea salt

60 ml (¼ cup) fresh parsley, finely chopped

2 ml (¼ tsp) cumin, crushed

60 ml (¼ cup) toasted sesame seeds

a pinch of coarsely ground black pepper

60 ml (¼ cup) seeded and finely diced red pepper

60 ml (¼ cup) finely chopped spring onions

15 ml (1 Tbsp) freshly squeezed lemon juice

2 ml (¼ tsp) fructose

2 ml (¼ tsp) olive oil

2 cloves garlic, crushed

Preheat the oven to 180 ˚C (350 ˚F).

Spread the quinoa and chickpeas on a baking sheet and brush lightly with oil. Mix in the salt, parsley and cumin, and toast in the oven, stirring every 10 minutes, until golden and crispy.

Place into a bowl and stir in the sesame seeds, pepper, red peppers and spring onions. Stir in the lemon juice, fructose, oil and garlic.

Serve on a salad platter.

SERVES 4

SPINACH, LENTIL AND FETA SALAD

15 ml (1 Tbsp) olive oil
180 ml (¾ cup) finely diced onion
a pinch of sea salt
2 cloves garlic, crushed
60 ml (¼ cup) fresh coriander, finely chopped
a pinch of fructose
a pinch of ground leaf masala
a pinch of ground garam masala
a pinch of turmeric
1 bunch fresh spinach, finely sliced, washed and dried
250 ml (1 cup) cooked lentils (see page 74)
180 ml (¾ cup) crumbled feta cheese
60 ml (¼ cup) pecan nuts, thinly sliced lengthways

Heat the oil and fry the onion, salt and garlic on low until translucent. Add the coriander, fructose, masala spices and turmeric. Cover with a lid and simmer on low for about 5 minutes. Set aside.

Place the spinach and lentils into a bowl. Add the onion mixture and feta and toss to mix. Transfer to a salad bowl, sprinkle the pecans on top and serve.

SERVES 4

SALADS

TOFU

Tofu (soya bean curd), like soy sauce, and soya milk, is produced from fermented soya beans. Tofu has the advantage of being a versatile and healthy substitute for meat or cheese, providing the body with both protein and phyto-oestrogen. It is also high in calcium and vitamins, but low in fat and sodium. It has no cholesterol and is easy to digest. There are two kinds of tofu: firm tofu and soft (or silken) tofu. Tofu is similar to a dairy product in that it must be refrigerated and has a short shelf life. It should be stored immersed in water, and the water should be changed daily.

HOW TO MAKE YOUR OWN TOFU

Soak raw soya beans in water overnight, then drain. Grind the beans while pouring a little boiling water over them, then spoon the mash into boiling water, as you would do when making dumplings, and boil gently for about 10 minutes.

This stage of the process is crucial as a certain enzyme in the bean is broken down during this time. If the enzyme is not destroyed, the soy protein will not be digestible.

Filter the resulting slurry. The filtered liquid is soya milk, and the pulp can be mixed with flour to make bread.

Add a small amount of either calcium sulfate or magnesium chloride to coagulate the milk. The Chinese have used the calcium salt, mined from mountain quarries, for 2 000 years; the salt is the pure form of gypsum. The Japanese traditionally use sea salt to coagulate the milk, and it is the small quantity of magnesium chloride in sea salt that does the trick.

After the coagulant has been introduced, the milk will separate into curds and whey. The curds will float to the top and the resulting whey (the liquid) should be clear.

Gently scoop the curds off the top of the whey and place into a forming container lined with cheesecloth. A forming container has many small holes in it to allow left-over whey to drain. Place a lid on the forming container, top with a small weight and leave to stand for several hours.

The resulting block of tofu should be transfered into a tub of cold water and left to stand for another hour.

After this, the tofu is ready to eat.

BROCCOLI, TOFU AND SESAME BAKE

30 ml (2 Tbsp) toasted sesame oil
1 large onion, finely diced
2 medium cloves garlic, crushed
a pinch of sea salt
500 ml (2 cups) fresh broccoli, chopped into small florets
4 blocks fresh tofu (about 100 g each)
180 ml (¾ cup) toasted sesame seeds
1 cm piece fresh peeled ginger
a pinch of fructose

Preheat the oven to 180 °C (350 °F).

Heat the oil in a frying pan, then add the onion, garlic and salt. Fry over low heat until translucent. Remove from heat and set aside.

Blanch the broccoli and drain.

Crumble the tofu into a bowl. Add the broccoli, fried onions and 125 ml (½ cup) sesame seeds and mix. Grate the ginger and squeeze the juice from the pulp into the bowl. Add the fructose and mix.

Lightly grease a baking dish. Add the tofu mixture and press it down into the dish. Bake for approximately 20 minutes. Drain any excess water emitted by the tofu, sprinkle the remaining sesame seeds on top and return to the oven until golden.

Serve hot with short-grain brown rice.

SERVES 4

TOFU, TOMATO, PEPPER AND AUBERGINE BAKE

4 blocks tofu (about 100 g each)

3 large ripe tomatoes

2 medium onions, peeled

2 medium aubergines (brinjals)

2 large green peppers

fresh basil leaves

2 cloves garlic

60 ml (¼ cup) olive oil for brushing vegetables and tofu

a pinch of sea salt

a pinch of coarsely ground black pepper

30 ml (2 Tbsp) freshly squeezed lemon juice

a pinch of fructose

Preheat the oven to 180 °C (350 °F).

Slice the tofu into thin squares and leave on a wooden board to drain.

Slice the tomatoes, onions, aubergines and peppers into thin rings. Brush olive oil on a baking sheet and roast the aubergines until golden.

Arrange the tofu, tomatoes, onions, roasted aubergines, peppers and individual basil leaves in layers in a casserole dish, sprinking garlic between each layer and brushing each item lightly with olive oil. Sprinkle with a little salt and black pepper and bake for about 15 minutes.

Mix together the lemon juice and fructose. Pour it evenly over the contents of the casserole and continue to bake until golden (about 20 minutes).

Serve hot with basmati rice.

SERVES 4

TOFU

ROASTED TOFU AND VEGETABLE MASALA

4 blocks fresh tofu (about 100 g each)

60 ml (¼ cup) olive oil

2 medium cloves garlic, crushed

2 ml (¼ tsp) grated fresh ginger

a pinch of ground garam masala

a pinch of ground leaf masala

a pinch of ground cumin

a pinch of ground tandoori masala

a pinch of saffron

a pinch of sea salt

a pinch of fructose

2 medium carrots, peeled and diced

2 medium courgettes (baby marrows), diced

1 small onion, cubed

fresh coriander leaves, finely chopped

Preheat the oven to 180 °C (350 °F).

Cut the tofu into small cubes and leave on a wooden board to drain.

Blend the oil, garlic, ginger, spices, salt and fructose together in a blender.

Brush a baking sheet with a little of the oil mixture, then brush the remaining oil over individual pieces of the tofu and vegetables.

Sprinkle fresh coriander over the tofu and vegetables and roast until golden. Carefully turn and roast the other side until golden.

Serve hot with a grain of your choice (see pages 60–62).

SERVES 4

TOFU AND CASHEW THAI CURRY

4 blocks fresh tofu (about 100 g each)

180 ml (¾ cup) salted roasted cashews

a few fresh coriander leaves to garnish

THAI CURRY SAUCE

¼ fresh green chilli

¼ fresh red chilli

4 cloves garlic

½ small onion

3 ml (½ tsp) grated fresh peeled ginger

10 ml (2 tsp) fructose

10 ml (2 tsp) soy sauce

60 ml (¼ cup) fresh coriander leaves

2 ml (¼ tsp) fresh or dried lemon grass

250 ml (1 cup) coconut milk

Cut the tofu into cubes and leave on a wooden board to drain.

To make the sauce, blend all the ingredients except for the coconut milk. Heat the coconut milk in a small saucepan, then add the blended ingredients.

Slowly add the tofu, making sure it is swimming in the sauce. Cover the pot with a lid and let the tofu simmer on low for about 10 minutes.

Pour the tofu and sauce into a serving bowl and sprinkle over the cashew nuts and fresh coriander leaves.

Serve hot with a grain of your choice (see pages 60–62).

SERVES 4

TOFU IN LEEK, CELERY AND MUSHROOM CREAM SAUCE

4 blocks fresh tofu (about 100 g each)
30 ml (2 Tbsp) sunflower oil
180 ml (¾ cup) diced onion
2 medium cloves garlic, crushed
a pinch of sea salt
a pinch of coarsely ground black pepper
180 ml (¾ cup) diced celery
250 ml (1 cup) chopped leeks
500 ml (2 cups) chopped button mushrooms
15 ml (1 Tbsp) soy sauce
250 ml (1 cup) soya milk or cream
30 ml (2 Tbsp) chopped fresh parsley

Preheat the oven to 180 °C (350 °F).

Cut the tofu into cubes and leave on a wooden board to drain.

Heat the oil and fry the onion, garlic, salt and black pepper in a pan until the onion is translucent. Add the celery and leeks. Cover and cook on low until soft.

In a separate pan, cook the mushrooms with the soy sauce on low until all the liquid has evaporated.

Add the mushrooms to the leek mixture, then stir in the soya cream or milk. Place the tofu in a casserole dish and pour over the leek mixture. Bake for 15 minutes.

Garnish with parsley and serve hot with a grain of your choice (see pages 60–62).

SERVES 4

TOFU

SPINACH, LEEK AND TOFU CANNELLONI

15 ml (1 Tbsp) sunflower oil
1 medium onion, finely diced
a pinch of sea salt
a pinch of coarsely ground black pepper
a pinch of fresh or dried mixed herbs
2 bunches spinach, finely sliced and blanched
4 blocks fresh tofu (about 100 g each), crumbled
10 cannelloni tubes
chopped fresh parsley to garnish

LEEK SAUCE

1 bunch leeks, chopped and blanched
250 ml (1 cup) vegetable stock
250 ml (1 cup) soya cream
a pinch of dried or fresh sage

Preheat the oven to 180 °C (350 °F).

Heat the oil and fry the onion with salt, pepper and mixed herbs on low heat, stirring until the onion is translucent. Add the spinach and the crumbled tofu. Stir, then remove from heat. Transfer the mixture to a colander to drain.

In the meantime prepare the leek sauce. Blend the leeks with the stock, soya cream and sage. Pour some of the sauce into a casserole dish.

Stuff the cannelloni tubes with the spinach-tofu mixture and place them into the dish on top of the leek sauce. Pour the remaining sauce over the tubes, making sure they are all completely covered.

Bake for about 45 minutes until the pasta is soft. If the sauce is too thick, add more stock.

Garnish with chopped parsley and serve hot.

SERVES 4

VEGAN BOBOTIE

30 ml (2 Tbsp) soy sauce
5 ml (1 tsp) tomato paste
750 ml (3 cups) boiling hot soup stock
500 ml (2 cups) dehydrated soya mince
30 ml (2 Tbsp) sunflower oil
1 medium onion, finely diced
2 medium cloves garlic, crushed
30 ml (2 Tbsp) chopped fresh coriander
a pinch of turmeric
a pinch of ground garam masala
a pinch of leaf masala
a pinch of sea salt
a pinch of fructose
60 ml (¼ cup) raisins

TOPPING

1 block fresh tofu (about 100 g)
a pinch of turmeric
a pinch of fructose
a pinch of herb salt
180 ml (¾ cup) water
a pinch of paprika to garnish

Preheat the oven to 180 °C (350 °F).

Add the soy sauce and tomato paste to the stock and pour it over the soya mince, leaving it to soak for a while.

In a deep frying pan heat the oil and fry the onion, garlic, coriander, spices, salt and fructose on low until the onion is translucent. Add the raisins and the soya mince. Cover with a lid and simmer on low for a couple of minutes.

Remove the pan from the heat and pour its contents into a baking dish. Flatten out the mixture.

To prepare the topping, blend the tofu, turmeric, fructose, herb salt and water until it forms a smooth cream. Pour it over the mince mixture, spreading it evenly. Sprinkle some paprika over the top for colour and leave the dish at room temperature for about 15 minutes to set. Bake for 45 minutes and serve hot with basmati rice.

SERVES 4

TOFU

CURRIED VEGETABLE AND TOFU KEBABS

60 ml (¼ cup) peanut oil

60 ml (¼ cup) plum sauce or apple juice

5 ml (1 tsp) soy sauce

a pinch of turmeric

a pinch of garam masala

a pinch of ground leaf masala

a pinch of herb salt

2 ml (¼ tsp) crushed garlic

2 ml (¼ tsp) chopped fresh coriander

1 medium onion, cut into thin, bite-sized pieces

1 green pepper, seeded and cubed

1 red pepper, seeded and cubed

2 courgettes (baby marrows), sliced into rings

½ small butternut, peeled and cut into thin, bite-sized pieces

4 blocks fresh tofu (about 100 g each), cut into thin, bite-sized pieces

16 plump, dried apricots

4 slices fresh pineapple, cut into thin, bite-sized pieces

Blend the oil, sauces, spices, salt, garlic and coriander.

Arrange the vegetables, tofu and fruit in rows on the skewers. Brush them thoroughly with the oil mixture and grill or barbecue, turning regularly until all the ingredients are cooked and crispy. Serve hot.

SERVES 4

TOFU

TOFU TEMPURA

4 blocks fresh tofu (about 100 g each),
cut into medium-sized cubes
500 ml (2 cups) sunflower oil for deep-frying

TEMPURA BATTER

30 ml (2 Tbsp) millet flour
30 ml (2 Tbsp) brown rice flour
30 ml (2 Tbsp) white rice flour
30 ml (2 Tbsp) fine yellow maize meal
375 ml (1½ cups) potato flour
a pinch of herb salt
500 ml (2 cups) ice-cold, still mineral water
45 ml (3 Tbsp) sesame seeds

First make the batter by blending the flours, salt and water until smooth. The consistency needs to be somewhere between that of milk and cream. Pour the mixture into a bowl, add the sesame seeds and mix. Refrigerate for about 15 minutes.

Immerse the tofu pieces in the tempura batter, making sure that all the sides are completely covered. Deep-fry the tofu, then drain in a colander.

The tofu can be served hot or cold with a sweet-and-sour sauce or chutney.

SERVES 4

DEEP-FRIED TOFU WITH TOMATO-BASIL SAUCE

6 ripe tomatoes, skinned and quartered

180 ml (¾ cup) fresh basil leaves

15 ml (1 Tbsp) olive oil

1 medium onion, quartered

3 cloves garlic

a pinch of sea salt

a pinch of coarsely ground black pepper

10 ml (2 tsp) fructose

500 ml (2 cups) sunflower oil for deep-frying

4 blocks fresh tofu (about 100 g each), cubed

chopped fresh basil to garnish

Blend the tomatoes, basil, olive oil, onion, garlic, salt, pepper and fructose. Place the mixture into a saucepan and cook on low for about 1 hour.

In the meantime, heat the oil in a wok and, when very hot, plunge the tofu into the oil until it turns golden in colour. Lift it out immediately and place into a colander to drain.

Put the tofu cubes in a serving bowl. When the tomato sauce is cooked, pour it over the tofu and garnish with chopped basil.

This dish can be served hot with a grain of your choice (see pages 60–62), or cold as a salad.

SERVES 4

STEAMED TOFU WITH VEGETABLES AND SEAWEED

1 small head broccoli, cut into small florets

2 large carrots, peeled and sliced

1 medium onion, sliced lengthways

2 large courgettes (baby marrows), sliced

1 small head cauliflower, cut into small florets

5 ml (1 tsp) toasted sesame oil

a pinch of herb salt

a pinch of fructose

2 ml (¼ tsp) peeled and grated fresh ginger

3 ml (½ tsp) soy sauce

1 packet toasted nori sheets

4 blocks fresh tofu (about 100 g each)

60 ml (¼ cup) toasted sesame seeds to garnish

Blanch all the vegetables, drain and lightly toss in a bowl with the oil, herb salt, fructose, ginger and soy sauce.

Line a bamboo steamer with enough nori sheets to cover the surface. Place the blocks of tofu on top of the nori sheets and scatter the vegetables around and on top of the tofu.

Take half a nori sheet and cut it into thin strips with kitchen scissors. Sprinkle the shreds of nori on top of the vegetables and tofu.

Cover and steam for about 20 minutes.

Sprinkle with sesame seeds and serve hot with short-grain brown rice.

SERVES 4

57 TOFU

GRAINS

All grains consist of an outer covering or husk, an inner kernel, and a germ. Between the husk and the kernel are layers of bran, which contain vitamins and minerals. The inner kernel contains mainly starch and a little protein. The germ is where vitamins (especially vitamin E), protein, and fats are stored. When a grain is refined or processed the husk is removed. This causes it to lose the bran as well as parts of the kernel and germ. Thus, the more refined or processed a grain, the less its nutritional value.

Whole grains are among the richest sources of B vitamins, protein and calcium.

COOKING TIPS

All grains must be washed before cooking. Place the grain into a bowl, cover with water and let it stand for 3 minutes. Remove any debris floating on top of the water and rinse until the water is clear. Replace the water and begin the cooking process.

Cook the grain slowly to give it time to expand. If the grain remains at a high temperature for too long, the water will evaporate too quickly and the grain will be raw. The grain needs to be brought to the boil for a couple of minutes and then left to simmer slowly on low until there is no liquid left. Stir the grain with a fork rather than a spoon to prevent it from fragmenting. Leave the grain to stand for 10 minutes before fluffing.

Stainless-steel pots are ideal because they retain heat long after they have been removed from the stove. If the grain has lost its water too quickly and is not cooked properly (provided it is not totally raw), you can switch off the stove, leave the lid on and allow the grain to steam until it is fluffy.

Wheat-free grains include: buckwheat, rice, millet, rye, barley, groats

Gluten-free grains include: buckwheat, rice, millet, quinoa

HOW TO PREPARE GRAINS

1. SHORT-GRAIN BROWN RICE

Bring 1 part rice and 2½ parts water to the boil. Reduce heat immediately and leave to simmer until all the water has evaporated. Fluff with a fork and leave covered until ready to serve.

2. LONG-GRAIN BROWN RICE

Bring 1 part rice to 2 parts water to the boil. Reduce heat and leave to simmer until the water has evaporated. Fluff with a fork and leave covered.

3. WHITE BASMATI RICE

Soak 1 part rice to 2 parts water for 20 minutes. Rinse and replace the water. Bring to the boil, reduce heat and simmer until all the water has evaporated.

4. BROWN BASMATI RICE

Prepare in the same way as long-grain brown rice.

5. THAI FRAGRANT RICE

Bring 2½ parts water to the boil. Add 1 part rice and simmer until the water has evaporated.

6. JAPANESE SHORT-GRAIN RICE

Bring 2½ parts water and 1 part rice to the boil. Reduce heat and leave to simmer until the water has evaporated. Leave covered.

7. WILD RICE

Boil 1 part rice and 3 parts water for 10 minutes. Reduce heat and simmer until the water is absorbed.

GRAINS

8. BARLEY

Boil 1 part barley to 3 parts water for 15 minutes. Reduce heat and leave to simmer until the barley has absorbed all the water.

9. DEHUSKED BUCKWHEAT (KASHA)

Dehusked buckwheat is suitable for porridge and does not need to be soaked beforehand. Bring 1 part grain and 3 parts water to the boil, then reduce heat and simmer gently until all the liquid has evaporated.

10. BULGUR WHEAT (CRACKED WHEAT)

Bulgur wheat does not need to be cooked, only soaked in boiling water. Soak 1 part grain with 2 parts boiling, salted water and leave covered for about 20 minutes.

11. GROATS (WHOLE OATS)

Soak the grain overnight using 1 part groats and 2 parts water. Bring the soaking water to the boil and then simmer until all the water has evaporated or been absorbed by the grain.

12. RYE

Prepare in the same way as groats or whole-wheat.

13. DEHUSKED MILLET

Bring 2½ parts water to the boil. Add 1 part millet, stir and leave to simmer until all the water has been absorbed or has evaporated.

14. WHOLE-WHEAT

Soak the grain overnight using 1 part whole-wheat and 2 parts water. Bring the soaking water to the boil and then simmer until all the water has evaporated or been absorbed by the grain.

15. COUSCOUS (SEMOLINA)

Cover 1 part couscous with 1½ parts boiling water and cover with a lid for 15 minutes. Fluff with a fork.

16. QUINOA

Bring 1 part quinoa and 2½ parts water to the boil, then reduce heat immediately and simmer on low until all the water has evaporated. Add a pinch of salt and fluff with a fork.

GRAINS

MILLET, BUTTERNUT AND SPINACH BAKE

625 ml (2½ cups) soup stock
or 10 ml (2 tsp) soup stock powder
dissolved in 625 ml (2½ cups) water
250 ml (1 cup) dehusked millet
1 medium butternut
1 bunch spinach, thinly sliced
15 ml (1 Tbsp) sunflower oil
1 medium onion, finely diced
2 medium cloves garlic, finely minced
a pinch of sea salt
a pinch of coarsely ground black pepper
5 ml (1 tsp) fresh or dried sage
180 ml (¾ cup) cashew pieces

Preheat the oven to 180 °C (350 °F).

Bring the stock to the boil. Add the millet, cover with a lid and simmer on low until the water has evaporated. Set aside.

Place the whole butternut (with skin) in the oven and bake until soft. When cooked, remove the skin and pips and mash with a fork.

Blanch the spinach.

Heat the oil in a pan and fry the onion, garlic, salt, pepper, sage and cashews. When the onion is translucent, add the spinach and butternut and mix. Remove from heat.

Turn the millet into a bowl, then stir in the vegetable mixture. Transfer the mixture to a lightly greased baking dish, press down and level out with a fork. Bake for 20 minutes until golden.

SERVES 4

COURGETTE AND MACADAMIA NUT PILAF

250 ml (1 cup) basmati rice
500 ml (2 cups) water
10 ml (2 tsp) vegetable stock powder
15 ml (1 Tbsp) olive oil
1 large onion, finely diced
2 cloves garlic, finely minced
a pinch of sea salt
a pinch of coarsely ground black pepper
30 ml (1 Tbsp) finely chopped
fresh coriander or parsley
6 medium courgettes (baby marrows), finely diced
180 ml (¾ cup) roasted macadamia nuts,
finely chopped

Cook the rice with the vegetable stock as described on page 60.

Heat the oil and fry the onion, garlic, salt and pepper in a frying pan. When the onion is translucent, add the coriander or parsley and courgettes. When the courgettes are tender, stir in the macadamia nuts, and remove pan from heat. Add the cooked rice and mix lightly with a fork.

Transfer to a casserole dish and serve.

SERVES 4

SESAME, GINGER AND VEGETABLE STIR-FRIED BROWN RICE

250 ml (1 cup) short-grain brown rice,
cooked (see page 60)
500 ml (2 cups) water with 10 ml (2 tsp) herb salt
45 ml (3 Tbsp) toasted sesame oil
2 medium onions, finely diced
2 medium cloves garlic, finely minced
250 ml (1 cup) finely chopped spinach
125 ml (½ cup) chopped broccoli
125 ml (½ cup) grated carrot
125 ml (½ cup) grated courgettes (baby marrows)
1 thumb-sized piece peeled fresh ginger
10 ml (2 tsp) soy sauce
3 ml (½ tsp) fructose
60 ml (¼ cup) toasted sesame seeds

Heat the oil in a wok or a deep pan and fry the onions and garlic until translucent.

Blanch the spinach and broccoli and drain.

Add the carrots and courgettes to the onion-garlic mixture and stir-fry until they are tender but crispy. Add the spinach, broccoli and cooked rice and mix. Set aside.

Finely grate the ginger. Remove the pulp from the back of the grater and squeeze the juice from the pulp into the rice mixture. Add the soy sauce and fructose and stir thoroughly. Add the sesame seeds, mix, reheat and serve.

SERVES 4

CURRIED VEGETABLES AND RICE WITH GOAT CHEESE

250 ml (1 cup) basmati rice

625 ml (2½ cups) water

10 ml (2 tsp) vegetable stock powder

45 ml (3 Tbsp) olive oil

1 large onion, diced

4 medium cloves garlic, finely minced

60 ml (¼ cup) finely chopped fresh coriander

a pinch of sea salt

3 ml (½ tsp) ground cumin

3 ml (½ tsp) ground garam masala

3 ml (½ tsp) ground leaf masala

2 ml (¼ tsp) ground turmeric

a pinch of crushed, dried chillies

a pinch of fructose

250 ml (1 cup) peeled and diced carrots

250 ml (1 cup) diced courgettes (baby marrows)

250 ml (1 cup) fine green beans, cut into thirds

250 ml (1 cup) fresh cauliflower florets, cut into small pieces

125 ml (½ cup) crumbled goat milk feta cheese

60 ml (¼ cup) cashew pieces

Preheat the oven to 180 °C (350 °F).

Bring the rice, water and stock powder to the boil and simmer on low until all the liquid has evaporated. Cover and set aside.

Heat the oil and fry the onion, garlic, coriander and salt on low in a stainless-steel frying pan until the onion becomes translucent. Add the spices, chillies and fructose and mix. Cover and set aside.

Blanch the vegetables and place in a bowl. Mix in the curried onion mixture.

Fluff the rice and add to the vegetables. Add the feta and cashews and toss or mix lightly with a fork.

Transfer the mixture to a casserole dish and cover. Reheat in the oven for 10–15 minutes and serve.

SERVES 4

SPINACH AND FETA COUSCOUS BAKE

250 ml (1 cup) couscous
250 ml (1 cup) boiling water with
20 ml (4 tsp) soup stock added
750 ml (3 cups) finely chopped spinach
45 ml (3 Tbsp) olive oil
180 ml (¾ cup) finely diced onion
3 medium cloves garlic, finely minced
a pinch of sea salt
a pinch of coarsely ground black pepper
60 ml (¼ cup) finely chopped mixed nuts
180 ml (¾ cup) crumbled feta cheese
180 ml (¾ cup) grated mozzarella cheese
5 ml (1 tsp) fresh or dried mixed herbs

Preheat the oven to 180 °C (350 °F).

Place the couscous in a pot (preferably stainless-steel) and pour over the boiling water and soup stock. Cover and leave to stand for about 10 minutes. Remove the lid and gently separate the grains with a fork until it fluffs.

Blanch the spinach and squeeze out excess water.

Heat the oil in a pan and fry the onion, garlic, salt and pepper until golden. Add the mixed nuts and spinach. Stir together and remove from heat.

In a bowl, mix the couscous, the spinach mixture, the crumbled feta and grated mozzarella cheese. Transfer to a lightly greased baking dish. Press the mixture down, sprinkle with herbs and bake for about 15 minutes until golden.

SERVES 4

BROCCOLI AND BROWN RICE RISOTTO

250 ml (1 cup) short-grain brown rice
625 ml (2½ cups) soup stock or 10 ml (2 tsp) stock powder to 625 ml (2½ cups) water
45 ml (3 Tbsp) olive oil
1 large onion, finely diced
2 medium cloves garlic, crushed
3 ml (½ tsp) sea salt
3 ml (½ tsp) coarsely ground black pepper
30 ml (2 Tbsp) finely chopped fresh sage leaves
500 ml (2 cups) chopped fresh broccoli
180 ml (¾ cup) fresh cream
60 ml (¼ cup) freshly grated Parmesan cheese
60 ml (¼ cup) finely chopped flat leaf Italian parsley
60 ml (¼ cup) cashew pieces, toasted

Bring the rice and stock to the boil, then simmer on low until the water has evaporated.

Heat the oil in a pan and fry the onion, garlic, salt, pepper and sage on low until the onion is translucent. Set aside.

Blanch the broccoli and drain.

Stir the broccoli and onion mixture into the rice. Add the cream, Parmesan cheese, parsley and cashews and mix again. Reheat and serve.

SERVES 4

BASMATI RICE WITH BASIL PESTO

250 ml (1 cup) basmati rice
500 ml (2 cups) water
10 ml (2 tsp) soup stock powder
500 ml (2 cups) fresh basil
3 cloves garlic
a pinch of sea salt
a pinch of fructose
60 ml (¼ cup) olive oil
125 ml (½ cup) cashew pieces
1 large onion, finely diced
a pinch of coarsely ground black pepper
5 ml (1 tsp) freshly squeezed lemon juice
a handful of freshly grated Parmesan cheese (optional)

Bring the rice, water and stock powder to the boil and then simmer on low until all the liquid has evaporated. Cover and set aside.

Blend the basil, garlic, salt, fructose, 30 ml (2 Tbsp) olive oil and cashews until smooth.

Heat the remaining oil in a pan, add the onion and fry on low until translucent. Add the basil mixture and stir for a few minutes.

Fluff the rice, add the onion-basil mixture, pepper and lemon juice and mix lightly with a fork. Add Parmesan for a sharper flavour.

Reheat and serve.

SERVES 4

PULSES

Pulses, which include beans, peas and lentils, are a good source of most B vitamins (essential for both the nervous and digestive systems), high in protein, low in fat, and rich in iron, calcium and phosphorous.

COOKING TIPS

1. Spread the pulses out on a flat surface to check for any stones, then rinse in a sieve.

2. Soak the pulses for at least 12 hours (preferably overnight) to prepare them for cooking. When soaking, cover them with twice as much water as there are pulses – they will absorb the water and swell.

3. After soaking, the pulses can be boiled in the same water if preferred, as it retains all the nutrients (especially the B vitamins). Add more water if necessary.

4. Bring the pulses to the boil (on high for about 15 minutes), then reduce heat and simmer on low for 1–2 hours, depending on how old and dry they are (soya beans and chickpeas take the longest).

5. Salt should only be added once the pulses have begun to soften (in the last hour of cooking).

If it is added earlier it will slow down the softening process.

6. Add a strip of seaweed to the pulses while they are cooking to reduce flatulence after eating.

7. Pulses should always be cooked separately from other ingredients (and other pulses) as their respective cooking times differ. Only once they are soft should they be added to the dish that is being prepared.

8. If you forget to soak the pulses overnight, increase the ratio of water to pulse, pouring boiling water (from the kettle) into the pot and cooking the pulse at boiling point for at least 15 minutes and then letting it cook on low until the pulse softens.

9. You must keep an eye on the cooking process to prevent overcooking. After 45 minutes, keep prodding the pulse until it feels tender.

COMMONLY USED PULSES

1. ADZUKI BEANS
These are slightly sweet in taste, and can be used in salads, stews and casseroles.

2. BROAD BEANS
These are available in both fresh and dried forms. They have a nutty taste and can be served with lemon juice, garlic and olive oil, or in salads and savoury rice dishes.

3. BLACK-EYED BEANS
These beans are full of flavour and slightly aromatic. Black-eyed beans are particularly good in soups, stews, casseroles and savoury rice dishes.

4. BLACK BEANS
These have an earthy taste, and are particularly tasty in stews and curries. Black beans lose some of their colour when cooked.

PULSES

5. BUTTER BEANS

These are bland on their own, but absorb other flavours when served in soups, stews and curries.

6. CHICKPEAS

These have a nutty taste and are good in soups, stews, salads and spreads.

7. BROWN LENTILS

These have a nutty taste and are good in soups, curries, breyanis, patties and savoury rice dishes. They can also be sprouted and served in salads.

8. GREEN SPLIT PEAS

These have a nutty flavour and are good in soups.

9. HARICOT BEANS

These are bland in taste, but are good in soups and stews (especially those with a tomato sauce).

10. RED KIDNEY BEANS

These are rather bland, but are particularly good in soups and stews.

11. MUNG BEANS

These are slightly bitter when cooked. They are good when sprouted and served in salads.

12. RED LENTILS

These nutty-flavoured lentils soften quickly when cooked, and are good in soups.

13. SUGAR BEANS

These have a bland taste (like kidney beans) and are good in soups and stews.

14. SOYA BEANS

These have a milky taste and the highest protein content of all beans. They are good in soups, stews, patties, purées, pies, curries and savoury rice. Soya beans can also be served cold with a lemon and garlic dressing.

15. CHANA DAHL OR YELLOW SPLIT PEAS

These have a nutty taste and are especially good in soups and curries.

16. MUNG DAHL

These have a very earthy taste and are especially good in soups and curries.

17. GREEN LENTILS

These have a earthy taste and are good in soups, stews and curries, and can also be sprouted for salads.

PULSES

ADZUKI BEANS AND VEGETABLE NUT BAKE

250 ml (1 cup) adzuki beans (soaked overnight)

750 ml (3 cups) water

125 ml (½ cup) soup stock

30 ml (2 Tbsp) olive oil

1 medium onion, diced

30 ml (2 Tbsp) chopped fresh parsley

2 cloves garlic, crushed

a pinch of sea salt

125 ml (½ cup) diced table celery

125 ml (½ cup) peeled and diced carrots

125 ml (½ cup) diced courgettes (baby marrows)

60 ml (¼ cup) chopped mixed nuts

a pinch of dried sage

a pinch of coarsely ground black pepper

a pinch of fructose

Rinse the soaked beans and bring to the boil in the water, then leave to simmer on low for about 1 hour. Add the stock when the beans are half-cooked.

Preheat the oven to 180 ˚C (350 ˚F).

While waiting for the beans to cook, heat the oil and fry the onion, parsley, garlic and salt until the onion is translucent. Add the celery, carrots, courgettes, nuts, sage, pepper and fructose. Cover and cook on low until the vegetables are soft.

When all the ingredients are cooked, mix them together and place the mixture in a greased baking dish. Use a fork to spread the mixture evenly and then bake for about 20 minutes until a golden crust has formed on the top. Serve with a grain of your choice (see pages 60–62).

SERVES 4

CHICKPEA, PUMPKIN, WAKAME AND LEEK STEW

250 ml (1 cup) chickpeas (soaked overnight)

750 ml (3 cups) water

a pinch of salt

30 ml (2 Tbsp) toasted sesame oil

1 onion, finely diced

2 cloves garlic, crushed

250 ml (1 cup) chopped leeks

250 ml (1 cup) peeled, cubed pumpkin

30 ml (2 Tbsp) shredded wakame seaweed

250 ml (1 cup) soup stock or 5 ml (1 tsp) stock powder dissolved in 250 ml (1 cup) boiling water

a pinch of fructose

5 ml (1 tsp) soy sauce

Bring the chickpeas and water to the boil, then simmer on low until half-cooked. Add the salt and continue cooking until the chickpeas are tender.

Heat the oil and fry the onion and garlic until translucent. Add the leeks, pumpkin, wakame and soup stock. Cover and cook on low for about 20 minutes. Add the fructose and soy sauce when the vegetables are soft.

Strain the cooked chickpeas and add to the vegetables, leaving the dish to stand for a while before reheating and serving.

Serve with short-grain brown rice.

SERVES 4

BLACK-EYED BEAN PILAF

250 ml (1 cup) black-eyed beans (soaked overnight)

750 ml (3 cups) water

5 ml (1 tsp) sea salt

30 ml (2 Tbsp) olive oil

1 onion, finely diced

125 ml (½ cup) diced spring onion

2 cloves garlic, crushed

125 ml (½ cup) diced table celery

125 ml (½ cup) seeded and diced red peppers

125 ml (½ cup) seeded and diced green peppers

a pinch of salt

2 ml (¼ tsp) ground cumin

2 ml (¼ tsp) garam masala

2 ml (¼ tsp) ground leaf masala

a pinch of coarsely ground black pepper

30 ml (2 Tbsp) finely chopped fresh coriander

a pinch of fructose

500 ml (2 cups) cooked basmati rice (see page 60)

Bring the beans and water to the boil, then reduce heat and leave to simmer on low until the beans are half-cooked. Add the salt and continue to cook until the beans are tender. Drain.

Heat the oil in a pan and fry the onion, spring onion, garlic, celery, peppers and salt until the onion is translucent.

Add the spices, black pepper, coriander and fructose. Cover with a lid and cook on low for a further 10 minutes.

Add the rice and beans to the onion mixture and mix all the ingredients together gently with a fork. Reheat on low just before serving.

SERVES 4

PULSES

BLACK BEAN CHILLI

250 ml (1 cup) black beans
750 ml (3 cups) water
5 ml (1 tsp) sea salt
30 ml (2 Tbsp) olive oil
1 onion, finely diced
2 cloves garlic, crushed
a pinch of herb salt
a pinch of fructose
2 ml (¼ tsp) seeded and crushed fresh green chilli
2 medium ripe tomatoes, skinned and finely chopped
125 ml (½ cup) peeled and diced potato
60 ml (¼ cup) finely chopped fresh basil leaves

Bring the beans and water to the boil. Reduce heat and simmer on low until half-cooked. Add the salt and then continue the cooking process until the beans are tender.

Blend the olive oil, onion, garlic, herb salt, fructose and chilli. Heat in a pan over low heat for about 5 minutes. Add the tomatoes and potatoes. Cover and continue cooking on low until the potatoes are soft.

Drain the cooked beans and add them to the chilli mixture. Reheat just before serving.

Serve with basmati rice.

SERVES 4

LENTIL COTTAGE PIE

250 ml (1 cup) brown lentils (soaked overnight)

750 ml (3 cups) water

5 ml (1 tsp) sea salt

250 ml (1 cup) dehydrated soya mince

625 ml (2½ cups) boiling hot vegetable stock
or 10 ml (2 tsp) stock powder
dissolved in 625 ml (2½ cups) boiling water

30 ml (2 Tbsp) sunflower oil

125 ml (½ cup) diced onion

2 cloves garlic, crushed

5 ml (1 tsp) chopped fresh parsley

a pinch of herb salt

60 ml (¼ cup) finely grated carrot

60 ml (¼ cup) finely grated courgettes (baby marrows)

5 ml (1 tsp) tomato paste

5 ml (1 tsp) soy sauce

2 ml (¼ tsp) ground leaf masala

2 ml (¼ tsp) garam masala

2 ml (¼ tsp) dried sage

3 ml (½ tsp) fructose

4 medium potatoes, peeled and
boiled with a pinch of salt

a pinch of herb salt

125 ml (½ cup) soya milk

olive oil

chopped fresh parsley to garnish

Preheat the oven to 180 °C (350 °F).

Bring the lentils, water and salt to the boil, then reduce heat and simmer on low until tender.

Soak the soya mince in a bowl with the soup stock for about 15 minutes.

Heat the oil and fry the onion, garlic, parsley and herb salt until the onion is translucent. Add the carrot and courgettes. Cover and cook on low until the vegetables are soft. Add the tomato paste, soy sauce, spices, sage and fructose. Drain the lentils and add them and the mince to the vegetable mixture. Cover and set aside and leave covered.

Mash the potatoes, add the salt and soya milk and mix until smooth.

Grease a baking dish. Pour in the lentil mixture, and level it out. Spread the mashed potato over the top. Brush with olive oil and garnish with chopped parsley. Bake until the potato forms a golden crust.

SERVES 4

VEGETABLES

Vegetables contain a lot of water, vitamins and minerals. If they are cooked for too long, or with too much water, they lose both their taste and nutritional value. If they are cooked together with plenty of other vegetables, they may also lose their distinctive taste. I have therefore derived a method of separating ingredients so as to maintain each one's unique taste and flavour.

COOKING TIPS

1. Cook mushrooms separately in soy sauce.

2. Cook spinach separately by blanching.

3. Prepare sauce separately from cooked vegetables and pour it over just before serving.

ROASTED MASALA BUTTERNUT RINGS

1 large butternut, sliced into rings (do not peel)
15 ml (1 Tbsp) peanut oil
3 cloves garlic, crushed
60 ml (¼ cup) fresh coriander, finely chopped
2 ml (¼ tsp) herb salt
2 ml (¼ tsp) fructose
a pinch of ground leaf masala
a pinch of ground garam masala
fresh coriander leaves to garnish

Preheat the oven to 180 °C (350 °F).

Mix all the ingredients in a mixing bowl, making sure that the butternut is thoroughly covered with the oil and spices. Place the butternut rings on a baking sheet and roast until the butternut has turned golden and crispy. Turn the rings over halfway through roasting.

Arrange the butternut rings on a platter and garnish with fresh coriander leaves. Serve hot.

SERVES 4 (AS A SIDE DISH)

ROASTED MASALA POTATO WEDGES

15 ml (1 Tbsp) olive oil

4 large potatoes, washed and cut into thick wedges (do not peel)

3 cloves garlic, crushed

2 ml (¼ tsp) sea salt

2 ml (¼ tsp) ground garam masala

2 ml (¼ tsp) ground leaf masala

2 ml (¼ tsp) turmeric

15 ml (1 Tbsp) finely chopped fresh parsley

a pinch of fructose

chopped fresh parsley to garnish

Preheat the oven to 180 °C (350 °F).

Mix all the ingredients together in a mixing bowl, making sure the potatoes are thoroughly covered with the oil and spices.

Arrange the potato wedges on a baking sheet. Roast until the potatoes are soft inside but golden and crispy on the outside.

Arrange them on a platter and garnish with chopped parsley. Serve hot.

SERVES 4 (AS A SIDE DISH)

SPINACH TANDOORI WITH GOAT CHEESE

2 bunches fresh spinach, finely sliced
30 ml (2 Tbsp) sunflower oil
1 large onion, finely diced
3 large cloves garlic, crushed
2 ml (¼ tsp) sea salt
60 ml (¼ cup) fresh coriander, finely chopped
2 ml (¼ tsp) turmeric
2 ml (¼ tsp) ground garam masala
2 ml (¼ tsp) tandoori masala
2 ml (¼ tsp) ground leaf masala
250 ml (1 cup) goat ricotta cheese
60 ml (¼ cup) toasted pine nuts

Preheat the oven to 180 °C (350 °F).

Blanch the spinach in salted water. Drain and squeeze out excess water.

Heat the oil and fry the onion, garlic and salt until translucent. Stir in the coriander and spices. Cover and simmer over low heat for 10 minutes.

Add the spinach. Mix well, cover and let simmer in the spices on low for a further 10 minutes. Leave the spinach mixture to stand.

Stir in the ricotta cheese and transfer the mixture to a casserole dish. Sprinkle the toasted pine nuts on top.

Reheat in the oven for about 15 minutes just before serving.

Serve with basmati rice.

SERVES 4 (AS A SIDE DISH)

SOYA CREAM OF SPINACH, LEEK AND MUSHROOM

2 bunches fresh spinach, finely sliced
45 ml (3 Tbsp) sunflower oil
1 large onion, finely diced
2 cloves garlic, crushed
2 ml (¼ tsp) sea salt
1 bunch leeks, finely chopped
250 g fresh button mushrooms, finely chopped
30 ml (2 Tbsp) soy sauce
200 g fresh tofu
125 ml (½ cup) water
2 ml (¼ tsp) salt
a pinch of fructose

Preheat the oven to 180 °C (350 °F).

Blanch the spinach in salted water and drain.

Heat 30 ml (2 Tbsp) oil and fry the onion, garlic and salt until translucent. Add the leeks. Cover and simmer on low until the leeks are tender.

In another pan, fry the mushrooms on low in the remaining oil and soy sauce until all the liquid has evaporated. Add the spinach and mushrooms to the onion and leek mixture and mix well. Leave the mixture to stand for a while.

In the meantime, blend the tofu, water, salt and fructose in a blender until the mixture forms a smooth cream. Stir the cream into the vegetables. Transfer the mixture to a casserole dish and reheat in the oven for about 15 minutes just before serving.

SERVES 4 (AS A SIDE DISH)

GEM SQUASH AND MIXED HERB MOZZARELLA GRATIN

6 large gem squash, boiled
15 ml (1 Tbsp) sunflower oil
1 large onion, finely diced
2 ml (¼ tsp) sea salt
5 ml (1 tsp) fresh or dried mixed herbs
2 ml (¼ tsp) coarsely ground black pepper
375 ml (1½ cups) grated mozzarella cheese
60 ml (¼ cup) finely chopped fresh parsley to garnish

Preheat the oven to 180 °C (350 °F).

Remove the pips from the cooked squash and scoop out the remaining flesh into a colander to drain. Place in a bowl.

Heat the oil and fry the onion, salt and mixed herbs until the onion is translucent. Add the onion mixture, pepper and 250 ml (1 cup) of the mozzarella to the squash and mix. Spoon the mixture into a baking dish. Sprinkle the remaining cheese and parsley on top and bake for about 15 minutes, or until the cheese turns golden. Serve immediately.

SERVES 4 (AS A SIDE DISH)

VEGETABLES

ROASTED SWEET POTATOES WITH MACADAMIA NUT SAUCE

2 large sweet potatoes, washed and cubed
(do not peel)
sunflower oil for roasting
a pinch of herb salt

MACADAMIA NUT SAUCE

180 ml (¾ cup) toasted macadamia nuts, chopped
250 ml (1 cup) soya milk
1 clove garlic, crushed
3 ml (½ tsp) soy sauce
2 ml (¼ tsp) fructose
chopped fresh parsley to garnish

Preheat the oven to 180 °C (350 °F).

Arrange the sweet potatoes on a baking sheet, brush with oil, sprinkle with herb salt and roast until golden and crispy.

Blend the nuts, milk, garlic, soy sauce and fructose in a blender until it is smooth and creamy.

Place the potatoes in a serving dish. Pour over the nut sauce and garnish with parsley.

Reheat in the oven for about 15 minutes just before serving.

SERVES 4 (AS A SIDE DISH)

SPICY MIXED VEGETABLE AND SESAME TEMPURA

60 ml (¼ cup) brown rice flour

60 ml (¼ cup) white rice flour

60 ml (¼ cup) millet flour

60 ml (¼ cup) fine maize meal

500 ml (2 cups) potato flour

375 ml (1½ cups) ice-cold water

2 ml (¼ tsp) sea salt

2 ml (¼ tsp) ground leaf masala

2 ml (¼ tsp) ground garam masala

a pinch of fructose

2 cloves garlic, crushed

60 ml (¼ cup) sesame seeds

2 courgettes (baby marrows),
washed and cut into thick rings

2 carrots, peeled and cut into thick rings

6 cauliflower florets

6 broccoli florets

500 ml (2 cups) sunflower oil for deep-frying

Blend the flours, water, salt, spices, fructose and garlic in a blender. The texture needs to be one that is between that of milk and cream. (Add more ice water if too thick or more potato flour if too thin.)

Pour the mixture into a bowl and stir in the sesame seeds and the vegetables, making sure that they are fully covered in batter.

Pour the sunflower oil into a wok and heat until the oil is sizzling.

Turn the vegetables in batter into a colander before deep-frying to drain excess batter, then plunge them into the wok. Remove immediately once they turn golden. Place in a bowl lined with paper towel to drain the excess oil.

Serve immediately, or reheat in an oven at 180 °C (350 °F) for about 15 minutes just before serving.

SERVES 4 (AS A SIDE DISH)

VEGETABLES

POTATO, LEEK AND SPINACH BAKE

30 ml (2 Tbsp) olive oil

1 large onion, finely diced

2 ml (¼ tsp) herb salt

2 ml (¼ tsp) finely chopped fresh sage

2 cloves garlic, crushed

2 ml (¼ tsp) coarsely ground black pepper

250 ml (1 cup) finely chopped leeks

6 potatoes, peeled and boiled with
3 ml (½ tsp) sea salt

1 bunch spinach, finely chopped and
blanched in salted water

125 ml (½ cup) finely grated fresh pecorino cheese

Preheat the oven to 180 °C (350 °F).

Heat the oil and fry the onion, salt, sage and garlic until the onion is translucent. Add the black pepper and leeks. Cover and leave to cook on low until the leeks are tender.

Mash the potatoes in a large bowl. Add the spinach, the leek mixture and the pecorino cheese and mix thoroughly.

Spoon into a baking dish and bake for about 20 minutes until a golden, crispy topping has formed. Serve immediately.

SERVES 4 (AS A SIDE DISH)

VEGETABLES

NON-DAIRY MILK, CREAM AND BUTTER

MILK AND CREAM

COCONUT MILK AND CREAM

This comes from the pressings of the coconut flesh and is therefore dairy-free, but contains saturated fat. It is available in powder and liquid form and has a rich, creamy taste. It can be used in savoury sauces, curries or desserts. It will curdle if boiled and so should be simmered over low heat. Coconut cream is extracted from the first pressing of the coconut flesh.

SOYA MILK AND CREAM

This comes from parboiled soya beans. It is dairy-free and contains about 2% non-saturated fat. It is also high in phyto-estrogens. Soya milk is available in powder and liquid form, has a strong, beany taste and can be used in savoury and sweet sauces. To prevent curdling, simmer over low heat.

Soya cream can be made by blending fresh tofu with water in a liquidizer until it is smooth and creamy. The cream can be used for desserts by adding fructose and vanilla. Alternatively, you can use it in savoury dishes by adding salt, herbs and garlic. The ratio of tofu to water is about 300 g fresh tofu to 250 ml (1 cup) filtered water.

RICE MILK

This comes from parboiled rice and is gluten-free and dairy-free. Rice milk is low in non-saturated fat when in its raw, unadulterated state. It is available in powder as well as liquid form. It has a neutral taste and can be used in sauces, desserts, cereals and porridge. Simmer over low heat to prevent curdling.

OAT MILK

This comes from groats (whole oats) and is therefore wheat-free as well as dairy-free. Oat milk is low in fat and, in its raw, unadulterated state, is good for lowering cholestrol. It is available in powder as well as liquid form and has a milky taste. It can be used in sauces and desserts, cereals and porridge. Simmer over low heat to prevent curdling.

ALMOND MILK

This comes from blanched almonds and is therefore gluten-free as well as dairy-free. Almond milk contains non-saturated fats and is available in liquid form. It has a neutral taste when unflavoured and is best served as a cold, flavoured beverage.

NUT BUTTERS

Nut butters are usually made from blending dry roasted nuts with tiny amounts of oil until they form a smooth or crunchy paste. As nuts naturally contain a lot of their own oil, they only require minimal amounts of added oil to start the process. Nut butters can be used to make sauces. Delicious nut butters include cashew, almond, macadamia and hazel.

BASIC NUT BUTTER

375 ml (1½ cups) roasted nuts of your choice
(with or without skins)
a pinch of sea salt
60 ml (¼ cup) sunflower oil (preferably cold pressed)

Place the nuts and salt in a blender and spoon in 15 ml (1 Tbsp) oil at a time, blending the nuts on high speed until a paste begins to form. The more oil you add, the smoother the texture will be. Blend until the texture of your choice is achieved.

MAKES 250 ML (1 CUP)

CASHEW NUT SAUCE

250 ml (1 cup) soya milk
5 ml (1 tsp) stock powder
2 ml (¼ tsp) soy sauce
a pinch of fructose
180 ml (¾ cup) cashew nut butter

Pour the soya milk into a pan and simmer slowly over low heat. Add the stock powder, soy sauce and fructose.

Add the nut butter and keep stirring until the butter has melted and the mixture has turned into a creamy sauce.

The sauce can be poured over plain steamed vegetables or used as a gravy over a grain.

MAKES 425 ML (1¾ CUPS)

NON-DAIRY

CAROB, ALMOND AND HAZELNUT SPREAD

125 ml (½ cup) carob sucrose chunks
250 ml (1 cup) hazelnut butter
60 ml (¼ cup) soya milk
2 drops almond essence

Melt the carob in a double-boiler. Pour into a bowl and add the hazelnut butter, soya milk and almond essence. Mix thoroughly until smooth.

Spoon the spread into an air-tight glass jar and store at room temperature. This spread will keep for about 1 month.

Use as a flavouring for desserts, or spread over bread or toast.

MAKES 425 ML (1¾ CUPS)

NON-DAIRY

COCONUT RICE DESSERT

500 ml (2 cups) black sticky rice or Japanese short-grain white rice (soaked overnight)
1 litre (4 cups) water
2 fresh lime leaves
250 ml (1 cup) coconut cream
30 ml (2 Tbsp) brown sugar
a pinch of sea salt

Drain the water from the rice. Place the rice into a pot with 1 litre (4 cups) water. Cover and simmer over low heat until all the liquid has been absorbed. Add the lime leaves, then stir in the coconut cream, brown sugar and salt.

Cover and set aside for the flavours to develop. Remove the lime leaves before serving.

SERVES 4

CHOCOLATE ALMOND MILK

500 ml (2 cups) blanched almonds
1.25 litres (5 cups) filtered water
1 drop almond essence
a pinch of sea salt
30 ml (2 Tbsp) fructose
135 g (½ cup) chocolate or carob, broken into pieces

Blend the almonds and water in a liquidiser. Tie a piece of muslin cloth over a deep bowl, creating a dent in the middle, and pour the almond liquid through the cloth. The grit that remains on the cloth must be squeezed out into the bowl: turn the cloth into a bag and push the grit vigorously towards the bottom of the bag, forcing the remaining liquid to seep out from the bag into the bowl. The liquid that falls into the bowl is the milk.

Add the almond essence, salt and fructose. Melt the carob or chocolate in a double-boiler or in a pan over low heat and then add it to the milk and stir. Refrigerate for about 2 hours and serve chilled.

MAKES 1.25 LITRES (5 CUPS)

NON-DAIRY

NUTS AND SEEDS

Nuts and seeds vary in both their fat and nutritional content. They are very versatile and make wonderful accompaniments to all types of dishes.

SPRINKLES

SESAME SEEDS

These are a rich source of calcium, phosphorous and iron. They are great to sprinkle over rice and vegetables. To make the sprinkle, toast the sesame seeds on a baking sheet (ungreased) at 160 °C (325 °F), turning until golden.

LINSEED (FLAXSEED)

Linseed is mostly used for its laxative qualities. As a cold pressed oil it is a very important fatty acid, rich in Omega 3. The seeds can be toasted and sprinkled over salads.

PUMPKIN SEEDS

These are healthier when toasted. Toast seeds at 160 °C (325 °F) on an ungreased baking sheet. Keep turning until golden.

SUNFLOWER SEEDS

These are rich in vitamin B complex and have a higher proportion of magnesium than any other food. The seeds can be toasted on a baking sheet at 160 °C (325 °F) until golden. Sunflower seed oil is rich in vitamins A, D, E and linoleic acid. Ninety per cent of it is unsaturated fatty acid.

SESAME SALT (GOMASIO)

250 ml (1 cup) sesame seeds
5 ml (1 tsp) sea salt

Place the seeds and salt into a pan and toast over low heat, stirring all the time until golden. Remove from heat and then grind gently using a pestle and mortar to release the flavour.

This makes a tasty sprinkle for rice dishes and steamed vegetables.

Gomasio will keep for about 3 months.

MAKES 250 ML (1 CUP)

SOY ROASTED CASHEWS

500 ml (2 cups) dry-roasted cashew pieces

10 ml (2 tsp) soy sauce

Preheat the oven to 140 °C (275 °F).

Mix the cashews and soy sauce thoroughly in a bowl. Place them on a baking sheet and bake for about 15 minutes, turning until the nuts have absorbed all the liquid. Once they have cooled, place in an air-tight glass container. The cashews will keep for about 2 months.

Use as a sprinkle over salads, grains and steamed vegetables.

MAKES 500 ML (2 CUPS)

SOY ROASTED SEEDS

500 ml (2 cups) pumpkin or sunflower seeds

10 ml (2 tsp) soy sauce

Preheat the oven to 140 °C (275 °F).

Dry-roast the seeds on a baking sheet, turning often until they are golden in colour.

Remove from the oven and add the soy sauce. Stir thoroughly, making sure that the seeds are evenly coated. Depending on the desired saltiness, add more soy sauce for more flavour.

Return the seeds to the oven for a further 15 minutes, turning until all the liquid is absorbed and the seeds are dry and crispy.

Once they have cooled, place in an air-tight glass container. They will keep for about 2 months.

The seeds can be sprinkled over salads, grains and steamed vegetables.

MAKES 500 ML (2 CUPS)

NUTS AND SEEDS

SPICY GROUND NUT SPRINKLE

500 ml (2 cups) mixed nuts
2 ml (¼ tsp) ground garam masala
2 ml (¼ tsp) ground leaf masala
2 ml (¼ tsp) turmeric
2 ml (¼ tsp) sea salt
a pinch of ground ginger
60 ml (¼ cup) fresh coriander, finely chopped

Preheat the oven to 160 °C (325 °F).

Place all the ingredients into a blender and blend to a coarse powder.

Pour the powder into a baking dish and place in the oven, stirring often, until the nuts have toasted and turned a golden colour. Once cool, pour into an air-tight glass container and keep refrigerated for up to 1 month.

Sprinkle over plain vegetables or grains.

MAKES 500 ML (2 CUPS)

GROUND NUT AND HERB SPRINKLE

500 ml (2 cups) mixed nuts
2 ml (¼ tsp) sea salt
5 ml (1 tsp) dried rosemary
2 ml (¼ tsp) garlic flakes
2 ml (¼ tsp) dried origanum
a pinch of coarsely ground black pepper

Preheat the oven to 160 °C (325 °F).

Place all the ingredients into a blender and blend to a coarse powder.

Pour the powder into a baking dish and place in the oven, stirring often, until the mixture has turned golden in colour and crispy in texture. Once cool, pour into an air-tight container and keep refrigerated for up to 1 month.

Sprinkle over vegetables or grains.

MAKES 500 ML (2 CUPS)

CAKES

COURGETTE CAKE
WITH LEMON ICING

3 free-range eggs
375 ml (1½ cups) brown sugar
250 ml (1 cup) sunflower oil
375 ml (1½ cups) finely grated or diced courgettes
(baby marrows)
250 ml (1 cup) chopped walnuts
375 ml (1½ cups) self-raising flour
375 ml (1½ cups) cake flour

LEMON ICING

375 ml (1½ cups) icing sugar
5 ml (1 tsp) sunflower oil
grated rind of 1 lemon
freshly squeezed juice of ½ lemon
60 ml (¼ cup) crushed pecan nuts for sprinkling

Preheat the oven to 160 °C (325 °F). Grease a loaf tin (15 x 35 cm) and line with well-greased paper.

Using an electric beater, beat the eggs, sugar and oil in a large mixing bowl. Stir in the courgettes and walnuts. Sift the flours and slowly add to the courgette mixture, stirring thoroughly.

Pour the cake mixture into the tin and spread evenly. Bake for about 1½ hrs. Leave the cake to stand for 5 minutes before turning it out onto a wire rack to cool.

To prepare the icing, cream all the ingredients, except the pecan nuts, in a mixing bowl with an electric beater or a whisk.

When the cake has cooled completely, pour the icing over and sprinkle with crushed pecan nuts.

PAPAYA AND BANANA CAKE WITH VANILLA ICING

180 ml (¾ cup) sunflower oil
180 ml (¾ cup) castor sugar
2 free-range eggs
125 ml (½ cup) mashed overripe banana
125 ml (½ cup) chopped fresh papaya (papaw)
375 ml (1½ cups) self-raising flour
125 ml (½ cup) desiccated coconut
60 ml (¼ cup) soya milk

VANILLA ICING

375 ml (1½ cups) icing sugar
5 ml (1 tsp) sunflower oil
3 drops vanilla essence
180 ml (¾ cup) soya milk
60 ml (¼ cup) desiccated coconut to sprinkle

Preheat the oven to 180 °C (350 °F). Grease a medium-sized round cake tin.

Using an electric beater, beat the oil and sugar in a mixing bowl until pale and creamy. Beat in the eggs one at a time. Stir in the banana and papaya. Add the flour, coconut and milk in batches and keep stirring until the mixture is smooth. Pour the mixture into the cake tin and spread evenly. Bake for about 1 hour. Wait for about 5 minutes before turning the cake out onto a wire rack to cool.

To prepare the icing, cream all the ingredients, except the coconut, adding 15 ml (1 Tbsp) milk at a time until a thickish paste forms.

When the cake has cooled completely, spread the icing over and sprinkle with desiccated coconut.

PUMPKIN AND DATE CAKE WITH ORANGE ICING

180 ml (¾ cup) castor sugar
250 ml (1 cup) sunflower oil
5 ml (1 tsp) grated orange rind
2 free-range eggs (or 10 ml (2 tsp) egg replacer
powder mixed with 60 ml (¼ cup) water)
250 ml (1 cup) chopped dates
125 ml (½ cup) desiccated coconut
125 ml (½ cup) cooked mashed pumpkin (cold)
500 ml (2 cups) self-raising flour
125 ml (½ cup) soya milk

ORANGE ICING

375 ml (1½ cups) icing sugar
5 ml (1 tsp) sunflower oil
grated rind of 1 orange
freshly squeezed orange juice of ½ orange
60 ml (¼ cup) crushed pecan nuts to sprinkle

Preheat the oven to 180 °C (350 °F). Grease a 19 cm deep cake tin and line with paper.

Using an electric beater, beat the sugar, oil and orange rind in a large mixing bowl until the mixture is light and fluffy. Beat in the eggs, then stir in the dates, coconut and pumpkin, and half the sifted flour and milk. Stir in the remaining flour and milk and mix until a smooth batter has formed.

Pour the mixture into the cake tin and spread evenly. Bake for about 1¼ hours. Leave the cake to stand for 5 minutes before turning out onto a wire rack to cool.

To prepare the icing, cream all the ingredients, except the pecan nuts, using an electric beater or whisk. When the cake has cooled completely, spread the icing over and sprinkle with pecan nuts.

CAKES

WHEAT-FREE MUFFINS

250 ml (1 cup) sunflower oil
6 ripe bananas
125 ml (½ cup) fructose
125 ml (½ cup) rye flour
250 ml (1 cup) oat bran
250 ml (1 cup) potato flour
500 ml (2 cups) oatmeal
20 ml (4 tsp) baking powder
5 ml (1 tsp) bicarbonate of soda
10 ml (2 tsp) ground cinnamon

Preheat the oven to 180 °C (350 °F). Grease a 12-muffin baking pan.

Place the oil, bananas and fructose into a blender and mix well. Place all the remaining ingredients into a large mixing bowl, add the banana mixture and mix well. Pour into the muffin pan and bake for 45 minutes until golden brown. Turn out onto a wire rack to cool.

MAKES 12 MUFFINS

CHOCOLATE BROWNIES

175 g (1 cup) fructose
250 ml (1 cup) sunflower oil
2 free-range eggs, beaten or 10 ml (2 tsp) egg
replacer powder mixed with 60 ml (¼ cup) water
5 ml (1 tsp) vanilla essence
25 g (½ cup) cocoa powder
75 g (¾ cup) cake flour
1 ml (¼ tsp) salt
75 g (¾ cup) chopped walnuts

CHOCOLATE ICING

375 ml (1½ cups) icing sugar
5 ml (1 tsp) sunflower oil
125 ml (½ cup) cocoa powder
250 ml (1 cup) soya milk

Preheat the oven to 180 °C (350 °F). Grease a shallow baking pan (30 x 20 cm).

Using an electric beater or a whisk, mix the fructose and oil in a mixing bowl. Add the eggs one at a time (or the egg replacer if using). Add the vanilla essence and stir until the ingredients are well mixed. Add the cocoa powder, flour and salt and mix well. Stir in the walnuts and pour the mixture into the baking pan.

Bake for 15 minutes. Set aside to cool and to allow the baked mixture to harden.

To prepare the icing, cream all the ingredients together in a mixing bowl with an electric beater or a whisk until smooth.

When the brownies have cooled completely, spread the icing over, then place in the refrigerator for the icing to set. Cut the brownies into squares.

MAKES 12 BROWNIES

FOOD FACTS

A balanced diet should ensure that the following nutrients are ingested daily in moderation:

PROTEIN

Meat, fish, eggs, dairy products, soya beans, peanuts and whole grain (brown rice and millet) are all rich sources of protein.

FIBRE

Oat bran, fruit, grains, cereals, whole grain flour and wheatgerm are all rich sources of fibre.

SUGAR

Fruit, carrots, butternut, beetroot, molasses, raw sugar and honey all contain sugar.

CARBOHYDRATES

Potatoes, butternut, grains, turnips and parsnips are all rich in carbohydrates.

FATS

Use cold pressed oils containing non-saturated fats (unheated olive, sesame and sunflower oil) and essential fatty acids (linseed oil and safflower oil). However, when you heat oil (for frying, roasting, etc.), it converts the non-saturated fats to saturated fats. Therefore, cooking with cold-pressed oils for nutritional purposes is a futile exercise.

GREEN, YELLOW AND WHITE VEGETABLES

Green vegetables are high in B Complex vitamins. Yellow vegetables are high in carbohydrates and sugar. White vegetables are high in potassium and carbohydrates.

VITAMINS AND MINERALS

Vitamin A occurs in two forms: preformed vitamin A, or retinol, is found only in foods of animal origin, and provitamin A, or carotene, is found in foods of both plant and animal origin.

Vitamin A is an anti-oxidant (it raises immunity to help fight infection). It also helps to counteract night-blindness, weak eyesight, and many other eye disorders, and promotes growth and healthy skin, teeth and gums.

Vitamin A occurs in fish, liver, egg yolks, butter, cream, green leafy vegetables and yellow vegetables.

Vitamin B1 (thiamine) promotes growth and maintains the nervous system, muscles and heart function. It can be used in the treatment of the *herpes zoster* virus and also aids digestion, especially of carbohydrates.

Vitamin B1 is found in brewers yeast, whole grain, liver, nuts, bran, milk, legumes and potatoes.

Vitamin B2 (riboflavin) aids reproduction and growth, and functions with other substances to metabolise carbohydrates, fats and proteins.

It is found in milk, liver, yeast, cheese, fish, eggs and green leafy vegetables.

Vitamin B3 (niacin or nicotinamide) helps reduce cholesterol, is a prophylactic for migraine headaches, and promotes healthy digestion. It is good for circulation and reduces high blood pressure.

Vitamin B3 is found in liver, lean red meat, white meat of poultry, whole-wheat products, brewers yeast, wheatgerm, fish, eggs, peanuts, avocados, dates, figs and prunes.

Vitamin B5 (calcium pantothenate or pantothenic acid) builds antibodies, and aids in the healing of wounds and post-operative shock.

It is found in red meat, chicken, liver, whole grains, wheatgerm, bran, green vegetables, nuts, brewers yeast and crude molasses.

Vitamin B6 (pyridoxene) assimilates protein and fat. It is used for treating nausea, especially morning sickness, and various nerve-related disorders. It is also good for night muscle spasms and leg cramps.

It is found in brewers yeast, wheat bran, wheatgerm, liver, cabbage, crude molasses, milk and eggs.

Vitamin B12 regenerates red blood cells, thereby preventing anaemia. It also helps to maintain a healthy nervous system.

It is found in liver, beef, eggs, milk and cheese.

Vitamin C (ascorbic acid) is good for healing wounds, burns and bleeding gums, and prevents many types of viral and bacterial infections. It also helps decrease blood cholesterol.

Vitamin C is found in citrus fruits, berries, green and leafy vegetables, tomatoes, cauliflower, sweet potatoes and potatoes.

Vitamin D acts as an anti-oxidant together with vitamins A and C, aids in assimilating vitamin A, and helps in the treatment of conjunctivitis. It also helps the body utilize calcium and phosphorous, which are necessary for the development of strong bones and teeth.

Vitamin D is found in liver, oils, salmon, herrings, sardines, tuna and dairy products.

Vitamin E (tocopherol) prevents and dissolves blood clots, and prevents thick scar formation.

Vitamin E is found in wheatgerm, soya beans, vegetable oils, broccoli, Brussels sprouts, green leafy vegetables, spinach, whole-wheat, whole grain cereal and eggs.

FOOD FACTS

Vitamin K assists in preventing haemorrhaging and internal bleeding. It also plays a role in reducing excessive menstrual flow and promotes proper blood clotting.

Vitamin K is found in yoghurt, alfalfa, egg yolks, safflower oil, soya bean oil, fish liver oils, kelp and green leafy vegetables.

Calcium helps to maintain strong bones and teeth, metabolizes iron, and regulates heartbeat.

It is found in milk products, soya beans, salmon, sardines, sesame seeds, peanuts, sunflower seeds, dried beans and green vegetables.

Iron aids growth, cures and prevents iron-deficiency anaemia, prevents fatigue and promotes resistance to disease and infections.

Iron is found in liver, dried peaches, red meat, egg yolks, oysters, nuts, beans, asparagus, molasses and oatmeal.

Magnesium is essential for effective nerve and muscle function and helps the body absorb calcium. It helps promote a healthy cardiovascular system, treats muscle cramps and fights depression.

It is found in figs, lemons, grapefruit, yellow corn, nuts, seeds, green vegetables and apples.

Potassium helps to increase oxygen supply to the brain, assists in reducing blood pressure and in treating allergies.

Potassium is found in citrus fruits, watercress, green leafy vegetables, mint, sunflower seeds, bananas and potatoes.

Selenium promotes tissue elasticity and alleviates hot flushes and menopausal distress. It is also used as an anti-oxidant to neutralise certain carcinogens.

Selenium is found in wheatgerm, bran, tuna, onions, tomatoes and broccoli.

Zinc promotes growth and mental alertness, helps to combat infertility and prostate problems, and aids the treatment of internal and external wounds.

It is found in steak and lamb chops, wheatgerm, brewers yeast, pumpkin seeds, eggs and mustard.

INDEX